MW01100709

LONDINIUM POETA

verses from the inner city
1980-2000

by

Stuart Newton

www.emp3books.com

Published in August 2009 by emp3books,
Kiln Workshops, Pilcot Road, Crookham Village,
Fleet, Hampshire, GU51 5RY, England

The *first edition* was published Feb/2000 by Weslond Books
And the *second edition* in Jan/2004 by WB

This new *third edition* is a re-written, revised version of the second edition

©Stuart Newton

The author asserts the moral right to be identified as the author of this work

ISBN-13: 978-1-907140-04-4

All rights reserved. No part of this publication may be reproduced, stored in a retrieval system, or transmitted, in any form or by any means, electronic, mechanical, photocopying, recording or otherwise without the prior written consent of the author.

www.emp3books.com

by the same author:

Whitlathe Walrus –1976/2002
Souter Steel --1984
The LacBird Poems --1995
Dotterel Dene --1998

Dedication

This volume is for Raymond Mooney -- my major encouragement -- teacher and friend, from West London

Contents

PREFACE

I was hesitant to write of London, because it overwhelms me and has been so well covered by Dickens and other writers. But a teacher friend encouraged me, after two short poems in March/99. So I tried a few more, to explore my own part of town. These poems are from two decades of residence at Nottinghill Gate; then written together one year, after considerable reluctance to begin such material. They are not an over-view; they are very much personal, local and timely.

I know the poems of Charles Bukowski, set in the Los Angeles metropolis; some of the slant in my poems leans towards his way. A.E.Housman wrote his Shropshire poems as a unified collection; I also attempted such a collusion of poems for a greater whole. Sandburg's poem, "Chicago", is a classic; the cadence and syntax begets the idea of a modern city. I applauded his achievement in No.10.

London has been a popular venue for a long time; very much entailing all aspects of life today, for residents/ visitors/ students... My friends accepted these poems like none before – from the big modern engine that is a city. And the city eventually brings out an inner landscape within people; which is, I hope, worth bringing into the light. The poems are free verse and development of the first-person persona, through greater circumstance – this is the essential 'lyric form'. The poems are not free of rhythm or form, only free of rime and meter; because these do not work well with the material I came to write. London requires stronger, tougher structures.

Sorry, I do not aspire to any poetic circle; my influences and aspirations seem to be very irregular. I have been a professional teacher a long time, mostly in schools and see little need to change this standing – it has sufficed.

I included, for the 'second edition', thirteen new poems written in Spring/2001, from another stay in town. I revised and extended the 'Notes' and made minor changes to many poems from the first edition.

Prologue

London is old and new, good/bad,
great and small – big equations -- and
tiny tensions dotting the place like seeds
upon the hill, like stars against the sky.
A rack of opportunities hold me back,
keep me down, make me flinch, start
me fidget… make you wince, set you to
itch, see us sweat…

It is rich and poor, work/play, dull and
vivid -- a few fixed colours but no fair
results -- surprising answers and hard
questions mist the air like cloud across
the night, like wind across the roofs.

This is the metaphysics of the city.

No. 2

I am in Dickens' town (like a tress-
passer). My own house is early 1800
and our street heavy with Victorian
facades.
His characters re-emerge in the faces here,
like show potatoes from the home patch.
Each day I pass set pieces of his theatre,
into night, under gas-style lamposts.
The garden alleys in Kensington village
are good short-cuts to the Kandy tea shop
and Old Curiosity shop; with cobble stones
featured for horses and old war cannons
set up as stopping posts at lane ends.
I plagiarized his city for my amusement;
defamed his streets and lifted his plots for
my own devices:
"Landlords rule in cruel fashion", I tell friends;
"kids are deprived and gentlemen still require
private clubs.
What's changed" I can say?
After 150 years (or more) -- why change!

No. 3

Let's say her name was 'Rose'. Well
it could be; how she stood out all night
like a cut flower, at our street corner
from evening till late (a full week) waiting
for 'johns'.

She arrived from Glasgow six years ago,
using a Gaelic burr once to get my attention.
I noticed her alright, in thigh-boots and skirt.
She did a parade/step activity on twenty yards
stretch of kerb; engaging every man who
approached, or peered at slowing cars.

In winter I almost felt sorry for her, with
cold damp night air, stepping past in my
coat and warm pants -- she still in the show
outfit for summer.

Rose was a cash customer at the store, also
known at the laundry where she washed and
got warm sometimes. A Persian neighbour
said he was offered ten pounds for her, back
of the car park, but gasped at the prospect;
we were relieved to hear of some resistance.

I noticed she smoked furiously and seemed
to be unhappy with her hair, the way it was
bleached and tied. By now she was a landmark,

like a familiar lamp-post or shop-sign -- accepted better than I was.

No. 4

I never knew we needed parks
so much till now in London town.
I cling to these spaces and join
them up on my trails round the day.
I met a wife and gals along the paths;
sought the summer-sun and waited
for winter-themes; read and talked,
ate/drank...
My child grows to demand excursions.
Park can respell: RAPK, RAKP -- KARP,
KRAP -- very unfair anagrams!
Instead we can say PAKR or PRAK.
I keep going to them
like it is church, like it is home;
and remember a lot of things,
or sit and remember nothing.
You can see everything each time:
the old on the benches full and tired;
youth at games on thick lawn turf;
babies in the air, flowers in the sun,
birds in the sky and those on water.

No. 5

She lay on the pavement, with dust
upon her face, cigarette ash on her hair.
It was March and windy,
so that she moved with the gusts like a leaf;
lifted up and moved three/four inches.
I stepped over her
on my way to Marylebone Road 'job search'
-- so was in a hurry
and could not stop to help, or pick her up.

Further down the street I checked my diary
and found her at the back, on another photo-
card, same pose/same phone number.
It was lovely colour and glossy (like a
porcelain piece) with some brief info details.

I was about to call her that evening,
until seeing her fallen the same morning;
and it was plain I was interested but
also perplexed.
After getting back home, I got to thinking:
'must we be proud to bear loneliness,
or do these two somehow go together'!?

No. 6

London is a 9 -- 5 town not a
city of pleasure or illumination.
It is 9 -- 5... Mon – Fri;
then a lot of exits to
greenbelts and ole'beam pubs.
These same people who came here
are the same ones who later exit,
relocate. The ones who stay inherit
the Elephant-an-Castle, Windsor
Arms and Bethnal Green; they have
their ways with heritage, albeit pie-
an-peas or Sat'day-night sing-a-long.
All the new people are let go
like a despondent relative,
not able to view it differently.
How can bungee-jumping replace darts,
or Acapulco Gold take over fags-an-beer!
How can 'The Joy of Sex' or 'The
Joy of Cooking', sell here!

No. 7

Even after a month, she was still smiling,
still beautiful; in the photo-card sitting on
the mantle next to his time-piece.
How could she look so happy, so decent,
on a call-girl card!
He continued to study her and considered
calling, like the card he kept from last year.
By month's end he knew her every detail
and some bio-info he coloured in for her.
Maybe she had already gone – back to
Thailand, or Vietnam, he thought.
He hoped she would go home again,
innocent/unscathed to her advantage;
because he thought to know her and care.

She had gone/changed; shortened her hair
and lengthened her skirt to get into post office
work; until she and her dog could find a
home together...
He had some means, she had love and
no means -- but still no connection.

No. 8

"Go to work. Go to work" -- is in the air
at am-rush hour when I join the subway to
my job. It is in the air for thousands of people
each day and their direction toward the centre;
great waves of wage earners funnelling
through the turnstiles like grain in a barn.
I could raise my elbows in the crowd and lift
up, ride along with the throng never touching
the ground. And could return the same way,
with no incident, no delays.
Like radials of a wheel: they come from
Hampstead, Bucks, Barking, Tooting, Acton
-- into the hub of the city.
We spring from urban nests for another day
at work, surging with our breakfast quota
and morning drill.
At pm-rush hour we are like used batteries,
stained and heavy in our places on the train;
glancing about, fidgeting with bags, holding
onto bits of reading.

Today I sat next to an accountant at his
papers and a typist at her holiday pages.
She was glaring at the photos to exclude
us luckless travelers; I was into my diary
and the accountant clicking his pen at us.
"Work is done. Work is done", is in the air
at pm-rush hour; when I use the bill-board

ads to picture my cool comforts of home,
as I lean against the solid uprights.
When I reach my front door it opens with
greetings from hinges and presents a whole
package of rest and refreshment: "Day is gone.
Day is gone".

No. 9

Her card still appears in the phone box,
on the High Street all summer long,
when he passes each week; where tourists
call, kids hide from rain and friends meet.
She looks her best (for everyone),
but has a new name, new number.
Everyone had moved on: tourists gone,
children at home -- except himself,
keeping to his slavish rounds of city
courses.

The photo is clear and bright
as it borders the call unit, like scraps
in a book or stamps on a card.
He examines others but is loyal to
the one he admirers.
After such level consideration he inhales
and decides, taking up the receiver:
"Hello Ray, new ansa-info, good juice!
Where are you? I will be late, am on the way.
Okay. -- surrounded by water, but not a drop
to drink -- suit yourself".
The girls watch him gasp with the input,
then go, as far as they can see...
This is another episode from a
true story.

No. 10

"City of the big shoulders" Sandburg said
of Chicago, "wicked and crooked".
Can we say the same about London town?
There was Wordsworth about Westminster,
Betjeman and Dickens with his portraits.
What can I say:
always zinging the queues, tricking the traffic,
hopping from one island park to another...
"Hog butcher -- tool maker" he added,
"fierce and brutal".
'Old and dusty' I can say --
'Historic curio for the world, smog maker,
theatre, monarchy and liberty.
Player with the nation's media speak, our
modern issues, with foreign states.
Dirty, loud and posturing;
city of the old shoulders.

They tell me you are wicked and I believe them;
for I have seen your homeless under the arches
luring the visitors.
They tell me you are crooked; yes it's true I have
seen the muggers rob and go free.
They tell me you are brutal; on the faces of old
and young I saw the marks of long despair.
Having answered so -- I can sneer back: a short
wary slugger set against the big new cities --
savage as a dog foaming for action, cunning as

a vain woman needing attentions.
Show me another city with solid head hailing in
pride, with commerce, heritage and language.
Greyheaded/ ruinations,
fashionable/ restoring.
City of the old shoulders/smart shoulders' --
I could say.

No. 11

"Hey!
Come over" and he waves from
across the street.
"Please,
get me a whisky"!
I see a broken man at a doorway,
waiting...
for help/ sympathy/ kindness/ whisky --
and
I am young/ fresh/ hopeful/ curious.
"No. You need coffee".
"...with whisky".
"No. With milk and sugar".
"Take this change -- go
right, then cross over, turn left".
"I know the place".

It was late afternoon, my way home from
school, walking along sunny avenues;
finding a new route through South-Ken maze;
enjoying my youth, free-time, healthy/happy.
He was tired/ worn/ desperate and angry --
two star-crossed subjects in a 'rotten' borough,
at a by-way off Earls Court.
I bring back a small tot of whisky and
some convenience coffee.
"Bring it upstairs, will you".

His bed-sit room was a clear testament of
neglect, a picture of depression, good
evidence of poverty.
"Sit down".
"I'm okay".
"Have a cup of tea".
"No thanks, it's okay, thanks anyway, not
thirsty, just had some"... and glanced the
mansion chamber I sat in, trying not to be
scared not to be selfish.

Then he resumed a position on the bed like
it loved him the more, missed him the most;
resting in compliance to his trap, his torment
always to be forsworn.
We had to decide about fear and ignorance or
tea and manners. Which was it -- and was he ill
or lonely, victim or villain!
Of course he told his story, he had to, like a
troubled mariner and I listen as timid guest;
take his tea, view his home, serve the coffee mix:
then struggle with a large dollop of wretchedness
we shared.

Outside I continued home like nothing happened,
as if the world was meant to be good and beautiful
away from his block.
'My time will come' I figured, trying to be fair;
'maybe I can learn from this' I thought, because
I was a teacher.

No. 12

They eat when it is time -- he eats
when hungry. It is either tea-time or
supper time; either an Indian brew
or cheese-an-cocoa.
There are tea rooms, lunch places and
dinner parties for the Kensington folk.
He tried such -- like chips on Friday,
burgers on Monday, toast in the morning
and sandwiches in summer.
But he was not getting it right.

They insisted on blue-ribbon stores,
he attend church with a school tie; that
he make an alliance with green charities,
a subscription to journals not mags.
After coaxing and friendly testing,
he still getting low scores in residence,
going to be losing his visa for the Royal
Borough. Maybe he'd have to move east
or to Hammersmith quarters... last seen
at Barons Court trying the Times paper
under his arm like a cricket bat.

No. 13

One free Saturday I followed my visitors
guide and boarded the bus to a listed
site --

Stepping into Dickens house was real;
you could see the old stove and chairs,
drapes and pictures faded and heavy --
a good set theatre scene, centre piece of
a Victorian street.

Going to Keats house in Hampstead next
Saturday, the same, going back in a direct
way to see his entailment; get a feel of the
place afforded him, an elegant lodging en
-route to the Heath.
I gathered up the pamphlets to confirm a
visit, but felt uncomfortable with my unfair
interest and disappointed with the mute
company I followed round the items set out,
because it was more sunny outside. It was
also real outside; a garden with the yew tree
where he wrote an 'Ode' and back lawns
where he dallied with Fanny.

Dickens lived here, on Doughty Street,
awakening early to race horses down the
front lane; going out to city thoroughfares
for his children in need, surveying the law

courts. He barely lived there, but did work
and write his journal serials.
I was compelled to visit a holy place where
good work is done, against all odds --
Every weekend included a visit that season to
mark out my literary territory, to step upon
my legacy, trampling my forbears.

No. 14

I got hit, just as I turned into a tunnel;
a bird hit my head in the subway.
It was a pigeon, which kept flying,
then turned down to find safe ground.
I was surprised but no damage done;
the bird too, as it gained the platform
amid travelers.
We were both upset and confused about
such a clash, deep under the streets;
because the bird must have descended
two levels of escalator and two side
tunnels (looking for exits). I often took
a hit to the ribs from travelers, but not
a hit to the head.
It could not be caught, I thought, when
continuing up the stairway I knew.
It would have to remain, no way out
for a sky creature… would have to adapt
like the rats and mice down there, other
creatures from above, which also got
caught in one of man's marvels –
the train world under green ground above.
The next day, same tunnel same time; I
saw no pigeon and no mice or rats. But
they were together now; off cruising long
sooty arches and foraging the bare tracks.

No. 15

The choir are a helpless mismatch; one
fat man, two ladies very grey, smokers
and teens, a ginger New-Yorker. They
shamble up the aisle to file into oak
screen pews --
then sing out like an enchanted host.
The priest looks disheveled, miscast;
but is eloquent as a Guild laureate.
The church occupies a sunless street; with
love and peace echoing in the empty portals.
I reclaim my rear place each week, like a
bad tempered badger, heaving and sighing
at my prayer book. Then follows an after
-noon stroll and leisure food at home.
This is England where a 'mad hatter's tea'
service presides for an hour, like the story
book. This is Sunday in London, when even
Lucifer quits for the day.

No. 16

Was is the art of London life? --
a black man sat on the road-side pavement,
covered himself with metal pots/pans;
a pile of kitchen ware around him.
Next week he would move round Portobello
Road to another place for the same display.

Pauline, an old lady dressed-up as lamb;
travels her home streets from Lansdowne
to Ladbroke Square, stepping out high,
like climbing up stairs.
She exhorts out loud; sometimes engaged
in fluid conversation with the most unlikely.

Then there's the 'whistling man' from
Observatory Gardens, 'Nigel' the walker
out of Trellick Towers and 'our lady of
the birds' at the Round Pond...
Every measure of life, every degree of sanity
finds a way here to the capitol; co-habiting a
lost lane, a hidden street or a vacant one.

No. 17

An unlikely day in Kensington Gardens;
near the palace, out for air --
I saw a fancy envelope on the grass verge;
it was a letter, with crown heading and
water-mark.
I could not resist opening:
July 25th

"Dear Mummy,
this is just a short note,
asking you to 'resign' your position
-- within the week!
You know I am ready to be king now,
I have done the course (served my time)
and even have a son and heir.
You might enjoy retirement (overseas)
and the Duke more free to say his piece.
Sorry, but I really made-up my mind;
so can say that if I have not received an
abdication document by the eleventh hour
of Thursday, a state of division will exist
between us --
I will depart these comfy shores and leave
for Australia; to begin a new life on some
nice bushland estate...
(No worries; I still have good contacts
from my stay before, if you remember?)
...henceforth to be known as the Prince of
New South Wales --

Respectfully,
Charles W.
P.S. I prefer sheep anyway".

I paused for thought and re-read;
tried to reconstruct events and replaced
the letter, then took from the envelope
again and again.
I was alone and confused;
but hesitated when a park policeman
cycled past on his duty rounds.
His red face looked at me standing
milk-bottle still upon their lawns,
on the family property --
myself also warranted as royal subject,
with a plum in my mouth...

No. 18

In summer
I have to swim and bowl at cricket;
to fancy myself made-over before
Autumn comes upon us --

I become a different creature with
arms like legs, straight and tireless;
my hands circle high to splash the
wake of water from my breaths...
how the cricket ball is delivered off
my fingers to the target between his
reflexes and the bat.

The swans out here also enjoy summer
attention -- they display their cygnets
and lap the water in flight, fixing all eyes
upon them.

In winter I hibernate.

No. 19

That lasting summer
in the same park, same corner, I found
another letter without trying; it was top-draw
stationery and read:

August 20th

"Charles,
        I write this from my ambo, over-seeing
a park I still retain for private pleasure, riding
and the like...
So nice to get a real letter,
I get so many faxes and memos these days.
We are all well; in fact the Duke and I quite
friendly at the moment on our rounds again
-- going over to Margaret's today (clearing out
her shells). Wish you could join us before you
head off abroad. You never told me how you
enjoyed it so much; I thought it was Queensland
and the roos you liked to paint?
After your letter I finally got down to that book
on architecture – quite surprising views for
a countryman, who seems retiring of
relatives!
You can come to tea next Sunday, at Windsor,
4:10pm (by the west gate if you must bring some-
one) and sign your book for us. We really have
to catch up – alright. R.S.V.P.
dearest wishes,
ER.

P.S. Mother says you must telephone about
her dog pedigree, the new bitch she has.
Please don't forget the family.

P.P.S. The PM will be contacting you
at a calendar lunch party; try to be moderate
and if you can't be happy, then be informed"!

I re-read to convince myself it was good
and replaced the letter. Later, also found a
first-class stamp and posted it on; glad to be
a lucky subject pure and simple.

No. 20

The taxis –
a heavy black mass running
across my paths, across all
the ways of my days.
Quiet and ugly, ugly and
dangerous; tearing past my
shins as I slip past to a park.
They are all driven, steered by
the same man –
a heavy Anglo with angry voice,
no patience; no time for the
traffic or interest in the way-
farers.

No. 21

We were scrounging the park on an off
-day. A grass corner at the Orangery had
small paper tickets among dry leaves and
near the broadwalk were cigarette ends.
John was with me for an afternoon, to see
how I found the royal letters – if he could
find something.
"Maybe it was Green Park, or St.James Park;
more action down there" as he stopped at
one of many benches.
I had no need to explain my park, my end
of Kensington. Besides it ought not to happen
again; family affairs are not public exercises.
We did find a free breeze and produced my
tea-flask with his jam rolls to rally our wanting
search; an early October outing for two loyal
stooges. What could go wrong in a open park,
in a royal city!
LA is the city of angels, Paris the city of light;
London is toy town, with puppet rulers/ raggedy
dolls/ tin soldiers/ upon painted sets… set in
motion by clockwork make-believe; it is magical
and comical, silly and daring.
By the end, before parting, John was making
notes for his booklet on heritage walks and trying
to interest me, fill me in. While I began sighing,
trying to vapourize a lot of dreams and cares.

No. 22

Five times
at the post office today;
one letter each time: get it!
Over to the store twice
for two loaves;
from an 8-am rise
till night falling.
Two teas at lunch and egg;
then a nap and some TV later.
Tomorrow, I'm out to work
and free.

No. 23

The Princess waved/smiled/gestured
at us, baby and me out again, walking –
it was our Kensington princess, the new
queen of hearts travelling past.
So I tried a snub because I lost my job
last term and losing my wife from the fall-
out; like a radiation effect (car already gone).
Not to effect the princess (not yet) in her
shiny car, slipping across the parkway to
a palace rear entrance, like a thief in
the night. Her escort/driver glared ahead,
while she scanned the window for punters,
more subjects for a new kind of royal –
on an open Saturday.
The baby had keen focus at that range (that
age), clenched soft fists from the push-chair,
foamed at the mouth and chortled like fish
in a pond; her sudden overflow of emotions
(poesy).
I remember everything my baby did first
time; this was first with the rich and famous;
next was walking, upon the same ground;
then talking -- equally aware of my first time
at a princely snub and first time in an empty
park with empty hopes.

No. 24

I saw a man grow old in a very short time
-- as we would before medicine, laundries,
central heating and cooked food -- way back
when men would constantly trek to find food
and water; before coats and hats, before home
and hearth -- exposed to the elements and
empty to any human warmth.
One day he took to the parks and streets;
a quiet handsome young man about 24-years
old I saw, with smart Oxford jacket.
Next year
I recognized him by the Bayswater fountains,
much changed. Life as we know it, shrank from
him with shame; the shame of great failures,
great waste; a notice he serves in mere presence.
He crossed my path to the drinking basin to
scare off children with his hair long and matted,
his features coarse and sore.
My last sighting, he was after cigarette butts
on the footpath and checking waste baskets.
He had fallen thru the modern world to a stone-
age period in full view of everyone, like a magic
trick.
I hope his mother is dead, that he never had a
book in him and he owes no one any money --

No. 25

God came to me, in the wicked city,
when my child strayed into the road;
and a big red bus stopped infront of her...
Yes, a big double-decker halted and waited
for someone to retrieve the child --
I jumped forward to pick her up and
step to safety.
I waved at the driver over my shoulder,
daring not to look at him -- in case it was
the very face of God looking out!

I continued down the side pavement,
shivering and shaking like jelly, trying
to rationalize the scene.
She got back in the buggy and bubbled
in song with our morning outing.

My day was ruined with guilt/nerves/shame...
Next week, the same spot, I waited for
another bus coming by;
it passed like a ship at sea, fully unconcerned
but moving.
I was a cup of jello without the spoon --
promising but useless.
Each time I had to wait for a red bus and
watch it passing; was it the same bus, same
driver, a different fool?!

No. 26

Death in London, like the movie says of
'Death in Venice', is shocking, raw and
untold --
The dog was following, unknown to the girls,
but could not dodge the traffic like them.
They made it across the road to stand beside
me on the footpath, giggling at their lucky
stupidity.
I was late for school, hurrying for the bell, as
I passed them on the corner. They were glad
to succeed at something in their dismal teens
in a dismal district.
They still giggled when seeing their dog chase
onto the highway lanes then take a full hit
(fracturing every bone rupturing every organ);
a loud crunching bang, at 8:30am Wednesday,
my heavy day of the week.
They giggled between gulps of panic they got
from seeing the dog dragging itself another two/
three feet with head high towards them, as
its body began convulsing and the driver was
out the truck watching it dying, like I could not.
I turned my eyes away, but heard the confused
responses of two foolish girls, now exposed and
going to be changed --
I learned nothing that day, just a brutal reminder
how stupid the world is, not just cruel and unfair.
I burst in the staffroom like I was late (not quite),

like I already had a bad class and needing coffee
and chat.
I could not think what the girls were doing when
meeting my first class and Year-8 were happy and
ready for poetry... how the boys at front were hum-
orous about books and handouts.

At first break I searched for Auden and his "Musee
des Beaux Arts" -- good teacher efforts at coping/
knowing, good/evil, beauty/horror...
Ultimately their dog showed-up the girls; the same
time the girls ended my quest my thirst for the world's
end -- that day when I became very full, had seen
enough.
The same night I turned off the news when it came
to tragedies of the day and documentary hour on
'Model suffering: here and abroad' --
Now I was going home, turning back for another
far journey to where I came from, unborn and
unfeeling.

No. 27

On our bench I talked to the father, an
Eastern gentleman; upon the pathway
I watched his little girl, going
on her skates up-an-down before us.
He explained, his wife a full academic
and himself unwell...
My situation also poor; but his child
was swimming well, playing the piano
and writing stories.
He was ill but happy (myself free of such),
when infront of us whizzed by a perfect
new start again in skirt and top,
so pretty so prized.

For an hour he talked and I watched,
as she kept trying/ falling/ racing;
maneuvering among the older ones
like a baby calf in the herd.
Her red skirt fluttered up like a flag,
a small royal flag, as she leaned
forward chin first into the purpose.
Her legs were bronzed but bruised with
the boots I helped off her doll feet --
'Thankyou', she returned in Kensington
school tones.
I held her knee and sensed the very future
from within, wild promises in her blood,
speed and distance from her limbs; as she

leapt from me to grasp her bag to drink.
She was a princess of the park, he was
her guardian -- could I be the seer!.

No. 28

God (again) was on the streets, saving
my bacon and keeping me straight.
At 6pm I was fully tired after school;
enjoying a walk home in summer PE-strip
and bag, tired and happy through dusty
Fulham streets.

I finally met a main road to cross; but
at the middle line, see a speeding motorcycle
heading for me --
when I stepped back it swayed the same way;
leaning forward was the same mistake.
I sensed the rider's look fixed upon me and
waited to be hit -- but the bike went past,
behind me.
Two on-lookers gasped out and shouted like
supporters viewing a lucky goal strike.
I was in shorts and T-shirt;
no averting a terrible tearing of wheel treads
at my thighs and middle, then the weight/shock
upon me --
I kept seeing the impact unfold like this
the rest of my way home.
So I nipped into the first green-park further on,
to walk with skaters, trikes, prams --
confirmed about my fate/purpose, my route
through a dangerous town.

No. 29

Three days after New Year's eve,
oh God --
it was cold brass-monkey weather --
and she dossed in a doorway covered
with a nice coat -- my wife's coat.
I had to hesitate
about my mistake with our old clothes bag
left out for charity.

Oh dear --
I had to decide on two evils: taking her warm
cover away, or fighting my wife next day.
A punishing winter exposure on our January
mean streets; I knew her as local vagrant
who hit me for change at the corner -- now
she rested under collected garments.
I knelt over her to take the coat hem, carefully
peeled it off her legs/feet -- but she rose up
and cried out in pain, "ah-ahhhh"!
"Sorry it's the wife's coat, my mistake" --
"Ahhhh"!
"She will be angry, will fight me, upset our
baby".
"Ahhhhh..."!
So I ran with the coat, back to the house --
But my wife had another coat and three hats,
six pairs of shoes/jeans, ten sweaters and a
pack-rat attitude -- I could no longer defend.

The girl in the doorway so close; 10-mins walk
from us.
To make up, I would take some coffee to her;
some change, food, a blanket -- she would laugh
out loud remembering the night before.
I could get her coffee the next week, get my wife
to be friends -- but she didn't, I didn't, we won't.
Next day I rush past her patch, going to work,
nervous of my boss this time; to see her at
an early-am cigarette with no such fears and
none of my options.

No. 30

"Talbot Court is over there;
but that's a block of flats you know
-- or Talbot Road is this way"!
"No, I want Talbot Gardens"?
"Nowhere this side of the High Street.
D'you mean Talbot Avenue; because
it is just over there", pointing with final
success!
"Why are they not all together"?
"You would have thought so!
How about Talbot Crescent which is two
exits further, past the crossing"?
"-- Leading to Talbot Lane and Talbot
Close -- as the signs say. Neat eh"!
"Ha-ha; good luck to you;
sorry, can't help anymore".
"I will be okay. Thankyou".
"Good"!

"Wait! Excuse me.
Do you live round here"?
"Yes, well..."
"I lost my map/city guide --
any idea if Gloucester Terrace is near
to Gloucester Place"?!

No. 31

Going to his client at Victoria was spooky,
because going past the Army/Navy store
reminded him of first coming to London,
years ago and trekking up Victoria Street;
passing the cathedral and checking buses
-- appearing same as then, no change;
as if waiting for him to return,
then exit the city.
The new pupil was on Horseferry Road, a
Georgian terrace leading to Westminster;
where he once stayed in a basic bare hostel.
A boy not unlike himself at that age –
restless and confused; another kind of return
for him.
Dust filled the roads as people emptied the
office buildings; same people different faces,
same day different date... same work but
different jobs. By 8pm dossers bed down
in doorway shelters, as if to shorten their
endless day.
He hoofed back via the park at lesson's end,
like years before; lost and afraid as pictured
in retail windows; anxious about the proximity
of destitution, the threat of vulgar realism --
and monumental stone fronts moving it seems
ever closer, to complete their takeover.

No. 32

Don't you know,
going to the 'chippie' can be misconstrued
-- I was escaping another torrid argument
at home, to walk the mean streets a winter
evening, heading to a fish shop on West-
bourne Grove's north side.

Two cops pulled me over to search for drugs
or something/anything --
It was at Whitelys emporium on Queensway
by mid evening. I appeared suspect/suspicious
to a pair of rookies on the beat...
Backed into a doorway; three men berating
each other, confusing legal duties for hormone
conflicts; night clashes of adrenalin like sentries
in the dark over no-man's land --
"Empty your pockets".
"What"!
It started to drizzle across the doorway,
to underscore the issues;
by-passers still paused and gazed at popular
theme strains, city tensions tearing across
the cold wet air.

It was thunder and lightning at the crossroads
of Bayswater and Nottinghill, when they got me
crying out in anguish like a wild animal in a leg-
hold trap under bullish headlights/footlights...

"I am losing my baby".
"Move on now, Sir".
"My baby", I cried!
"Move along, please".

I stagger the pavement like a vagrant drunk,
like a wounded creature trying for safe ground.
On-lookers wander off -- show over.
Cops strolled away -- bust finished.
Stars move-on behind smoky cloud screens --
unhappy with events in the street that night;
one tiny flash rippling out to the sky above,
to the heavens beyond.

No. 33

My alter-ego jumped in front of
a train. It was 8:30am going to work
late and I saw my alter-ego go under
the train wheels. It was West London,
with usual commuters and some reliable
witnesses – two saw another man
under a train last month (tax
time).
I could not stop it for it happened so
quickly; but a long while to clear up and
set-off again.
For a long time people are round the
train/body with pen/paper;
flat expressions and quiet mutterings.
I didn't see all this because I had gone
by then; gone on the next train, then
to work.
The same last week – wife ran away
-- I had to see my libido go under
a train; so that I'm scared to go down
the underground; because I have to see
this again, really feel it.
Next step is ego under the train,
then the body I suppose.
You don't just go straight out to kill
yourself under a moving train; there is
a system of events and small deaths
first.

Suicide is not an easy death but
a programme difficult to stop, when set
in motion, across the path of a speeding
train.

No. 34

She was a Mayfair girl, in
a great residence and expensive;
but I went every Saturday to
see her with those older men.
I looked up to her chandeliers
in the big room, tried
to fit in with the people and
not eat too much.

Today she was attended
by a serious woman in blue suit
and man in a tux.
I sat down with my nibbles-an-drink
edging closer to her charms,
nervous of the game shy of
the risk -- "Last bets please",
I heard and hesitated; because
I did not love her and she was not
beautiful -- we got: "twenty-eight
on the black".
She was Lady Luck; my Mayfair
girl was an in-door type, stayed up
all night, to deal her favours
sore and short.

No. 35

His early paper offered notices of alarm
(grades of reference) and TV scandal
of MP/sex/money... he followed as way out
of his own problems -- job/money/bills;
wishing to switch problems, upgrade them.
After another sweet coffee he stretched out
for a hike to the bank, a store, post-office
-- because they made a circle walk for
the afternoon.
His bush craft was superb,
but his luck dismal as the old moon.

That same night same news scandal
and next day variations upon the theme;
in front of him each time he got to his chair
after a good walkabout.
He was in post-modern London but
still a hunter/gatherer, having to live close
by signs and signals – waterholes and way-
posts, night-calls, dropzones, outstations…

He was not old not young, he was not poor
not rich, not lucky not safe -- habiting a bare
snug near the water's edge; usually waiting
his friends come by to visit,
because it was now Spring on the river.

Next week more news about the big players

and who got hit.
No chance him as a target (screened out unfit);
more chance to be trampled, upon crossing
byways/fairways, when viewing his territory at
full noon.
Every day our hero walked the edge, left his
patch, unknown and unfettered.

No. 36

Ever sat in barristers chambers, wasted
a good afternoon? -- not everyone will.
But no surprises, it is all very familiar
-- three pairs of shoes pointing inwards
I notice more than the faces.
The chairs creak like my own; I see dust
on a window and sweaty shirts; it could be
a pool room, a bar, but without the jokes.
People are either tired or in a rush;
they are either ugly or intelligent,
old or stupid.
Suddenly we remember last time and
he says something new and important
mid-way through the slowness.
My eyes have to go from one voice to
another, then to the shoes.
My hearing is fuzzy over the tedium,
and I hear myself speak like a college
seminar.
We request a drink, tea or something;
though we don't need one.
I want to be far away; to escape this dull
trap (they give countenance to it all).
Around us are secretaries and the like;
seeming to scream out, or laugh, just
beyond notice; because we are transfixed
and quiet, or important, in a way women
don't like.

Three men in Tudor premises at a 'post-
modern' drama; deciding the fates of two
females at another place, one a child.
We are here because of failure and the law
is a waste basket. But Law is from men
(again); ancient Greek men who also
presided in temple courtyards, in stuffy
chambers on sunny afternoons.

No. 37

My first fan letter was a hit;
because it said, "love from Marie"
on the photo I received, to show
my friends.
One throw-away studio shot of
a high fashion model landed in my
scrap book: glossy document of credit,
a chit to prize.
A week later I sent a book of poems
(in good faith) -- and waited...
To see her on TV news, in that black
dress at a gala event.
My student teacher shrank from me
at telling over am-coffee. He gasped
a rebuke at rumpled middle-school
staff losing it again.
But this was London, where cats and
such can look upon a queen.

No. 38

He stood on the platform unaware of pm
rush-hour; when I was tired and forlorn,
descending a full escalator to deliver me
at an ordained place behind the American.
He was taller than anyone, quiet and strong,
waiting calmly (in a small pond); because
he was from the wild west movies. Actor and
villain of the piece; from the famous coffee-
pot scene with Lee Marvin and the hoodlum
in 'Kiss me Deadly'. Now three feet away
in real life in gritty London.
"Who is Jack Elam" he said?
"Then -- we want Jack Elam.
Next is: we want a Jack Elam type!
Lastly: who was Jack Elam" he said
to George Plimpton about acting?
He was the ugly duckling of movies;
now a solid figure in front of me at Victoria
Station; tall, wide and handsome.
What brought him to town; where
was he going? The hotel first I suppose,
then stateside to his home on the range.
Myself -- back here tomorrow!

No. 39

Lots of celebs and stars in my part of town,
I see, in ordinary places at ordinary things.
Not all these are people I prize – except Lee
Remick I saw at Sloane Square. She,
beautiful with Monty Clift in Tennessee, with
Newman/Fonda in Oregon at logging!
"Miss Remick –
your films, really terrific"!
"Thankyou".
"Surprised you here, in England I mean"?
We continued in the queue at the Post Office
-- lunch time errands for teachers/workers/
actresses… talking normally.
"I am in school near here; it's okay for me".
"Lovely; what I should have done. We have two
teachers in the family"… normal/special like
it had to be; myself shy/bold like I never was;
talking/listening like I never could.
Monday today and long wait, a long nothing chat
for me and those ahead/behind – an audience
in London, a small live audience, because it was
not private time or private chat.
She looked real; tired and worried about postage
(in films calm and fair). Her hair was tinted and
she clasped her purse infront when I turned to exit
the premises.
"Thankyou for your time Miss Remick.
You too, Miss Remick.

Oh, my name"?
We all saw royal persons in passing, the rich and
famous around us like a lantern frieze; but I only
talked with Lee, as major talent from the Method
Studio.
The weather dull that day, an average week; but
London never like this; more like a 'black hole'
in the world attracting stars, heavenly bodies and
debris.

No. 40

Xmas fayre in London is special; I think of baby
Jesus, then a Dickens waif. There are also full
celebrations of wine/women/song, in the best
clubs -- and the worst!
Posting my xmas cards I saw a man lying on
the pavement; carried there by a bouncer of
our local gaming club.
I drew closer, upon my way, to see him well
dressed but badly fallen.
Just as I leaned over to speak wet snow began
-- he was full of eats, drink, proclaiming his loss
to anyone.
"Stay here wait for me", promising to be right back
I demanded he remain put and ran to post my cards
to run back.
He was a true Xmas figure of meekness and giving
-- more sleet fell onto the abject man onto his
muttering lips: "took all my money, my xmas bonus"
and explaining why getting wet/cold so could not
move to help himself -- "I can't go home, not
now".
I found five pounds in his pockets; money for a taxi
from the club I thought and we began to rise up to
walk.
He was rightly plaintive as we journeyed for a main
road, for a black cab. Three cabs would not take him
when the drivers heard my appeal -- then one did
and took his address. I cried "Please take him home,

please".

He made no protest as I fitted him onto the back seat
folding up his arms for the ride; clutching at his pockets
to check we were not mistaken (little chance tonight);
and becoming frightened of the woman at home I
could now see waiting.

There was no room at the Inn for Joseph at Xmas
and no room in the club for my friend. But Jesus was
born in a stable and love finds those on the street.

No. 41

I find another period terrace and Queen
Anne cottages, from this open sill.
Lunch time I see someone at the door
of one house and a postman leaving his
intrusions in the boxes.
The past looks appealing from here, like
London is appealing to visitors. While I
scuttle after a living then thread the walled
streets going home – guessing at life in
such residences -- trying to go backwards,
to see myself enact with habitants from
the past, but the interiors are dark and
empty.
I return to my class for pm tasks, yet still
want to go in, through the sash windows
behind facing bricks of a Regency terrace.
These wishes are strong; but those stones
can be stronger, holding out for hundreds
of years beyond my own life.
Stone can be a satisfying artifact when
worked to fit (rendered) and set with others;
adorned by blue wisteria, topped by blue-
gray slates. It is raised upon the dead past,
and lives longer.
My own area of London is Victorian; where
our big houses and heavy porticos will survive
to be restored and revalued; while I languish,
die, disappear…

From such building we both win and lose
-- we are diminished by the sheer mass;
at the same time we give it shape, make
it serve.

No. 42

I went round at 8pm for usual date and started
with tea and gossip. He found some biscuits
and set cups out to fill in the spare itinerary --
Chas coming at 9, two Eastern ladies maybe
at the bar by 10pm.
Two phone calls later I repaired to his lounge
with a hot whisky and ginger cake:
"Teaching is no fun anymore..."
"Maybe our fault -- as 'Three Men in a Boat', me, you
and Charles; browned crusty dumplings adrift in Earls
Court -- like 'Mister Polly' in a boat, with no paddles".
"That's alright. Having fun is all".
"Not for them --"
"Who"?
"The ones not in the boat; like our gal at the Internet
cafe".
"She's okay -- Brazil isn't it"!
"-- only fed up with us".
When I read out my new poems he closed his eyes,
expiring on a wide couch.
"Wake up", I insisted.
"I want to visualize it. Please go on".
"No, not a meditation to soothe you".
"Read it again".
"Wait, it's the door".
"Water, water, everywhere; nor any drop to drink"!
"I could be bound in a nutshell and count myself
king of infinite space; or joker in-the pack if you like".

"Enough"!

Next we re-formed round a table at the usual hotel; fussing over brew choices, warming-up the barmaid, and matching payments. Then retelling our favoured story items before checking the exits for the ladies entrance. No show, but more beer came, more table nuts, fueling a litany of men's musings.

This is a true story of another topping on our Friday evening segment.

No. 43

I was spinning with good-will (but sober)
from a lucky encounter that day --
A good target for a drunken man on the open
pavement lot at Edgware Station, where
enough by-passers can become an audience
for street live theatre.
He came at me legless and discredited; came
like a drowning man grasping straws.
"You had any bad knocks"?
"Not really".
He grabbed my gaze with his watery blue eyes
changing a strong grey to hold me there --
"You travelled a lot, have yeah"?
"Little bit".
For the next ten minutes he swayed at me,
wobbled and mumbled, while I tried to be
diplomatic. But there was a message within him
which could not come out; about weakness/fear
/loss; as he moved the very long handshake to
a desperate grasp of my arm/elbow, an embrace...
Because
his head was shaved and he was openly
vulnerable, I could see his mother's child with
-out her swathing bands, much for the pity of it.
He was another lost mariner (of the Coleridge
school) who had a tale to tell.
But he was in the city not at the coast -- like
a seafarer stranded from a big full-tide up

the Edgware river Road, by Paddington docks,
without a paddle's chance of help.

No. 44

I saw school children in my park,
about two hundred when crossing the field
corner, in ladybird uniform among the trees
like bugs upon a quilt – they were playing
some English games, with bat and ball
and teachers.
I jumped when their whistle blew and kept
walking when they ran.
After they were all seated, I stopped on
a bench and waited with them for the next
moves from teachers I saw standing straight
-up in control; myself lounging on a vacant
seat.
There were four groups playing and parents
bordering the events in happy quiet, like
a pastel picture.
It was July in London, the season of sports
when schools broke out of grounds to camp,
play or tour – as I was out
to make a living even in best weather.

Oh children look at me, oh God please watch
in passing – London has yet such children
and God will notice me upon my way.
I take out a diary to add things to my day,
important things; clasp it like a passport to
the next life like a prayer book and fill the pages
in hope in habit.

The children are already filled up;
every moment for them bursts upon the next,
in concert with each other.
From the bench I stepped onto a broadwalk,
to meet the skaters. I get into a central space
and enjoy going the opposite way, against
the stream.

Oh skaters watch-out for me, oh God watch me
among your park pranksters – because London
has currents and tides (newhappenstance),
floods of people and those going up-stream…
Next
I sight model yachts skim over ruffled pond water,
among swan pairs. It is late mating for high-white
birds gliding by and early chances for hobby craft
find the breeze – these also race with filling sails,
or fly on folding wings (an eclipse passes in
minutes); trekking the ground is long and slow.

No. 45

Four Indians with one squaw I met in
Kensington were happy at browsing.
I was amazed with Iroquois Indians from
Ontario in-an-out of shops on Queensway.
I followed about fifteen minutes before
speaking till I was sure --
they were on tour of Britain with music
and dance for the summer, going home
next week, home to the reservation range.
Lots of foreigners in W2 but these worried
by the glitz and show on the streets. They
were constantly chuckling and pointing;
but were glad to see me and shake on it,
when I said from Vancouver; then I began
pointing/chuckling everywhere.

Of course they never left Ontario before
and not sure of England or the crowds,
from the quick giggles; unsure of types
they saw and dizzy with the surrounds.
Finally one admitted -- "Just like Toronto
here, crazy place, really like Toronto"!
This seemed to bring it all into the open
on a short September afternoon.
I padded up the High Street, then turned
to go by underground -- I see them skipping
down the escalators like it was a pine bridge,
heading off to a hotel like

it was the long-house with smoke/fish.

No. 46

Coming round to Trebovir Road from
Nevern Square, we passed a street girl
leaning against the cars in short skirt/light
top, swinging a drink bottle.
There were two of us, but she went for me,
clinging onto my shyness; "come on, let's
share this wine".
She was at me like a hungry creature of
the forest -- I had no chance, except to ease
from her jaws as I went limp and slippery.
"You can catch up later" my friend left me
with at the corner.
"Come on, try some" got me tilting the bottle
high; but it was a feint to closed lips.
"Too sweet",
I said; as she caught my arm in close to show
a yellow tint in her eyes, her blistered cheeks
and seared brow --
already a ghost of a young woman, made to
haunt the red lights of Earls Court on Friday/
Saturday nights, amongst the silvery quick,
against the darkening horizons.
Reaching the main road she skipped into a
tavern for some 'coke', when I pared off to
a hotel bar and find him waiting on my turn
to buy. Then we hammered out how alcohol
and zygotes go together.

No. 47

"You look down" --
He sat in a corner seat, to watch what he
was trying to avoid, drank beer because
he wanted whisky.
"Good week"? --
tried his companion to start the evening.
The response was an annotated list,
some facial clues and loaded pauses.
"Hear about James"? --
his companion pressed home the advantage,
so he had to concede some inside info-juice
of news for a seasoned city palate;
or purchase the next round of elixir ales.
"Real smoky corner" --
He was blowing into his drink between gulps,
blowing and drowning in a special bitter brew.
"Getting too crowded" --
He was not new to this drinking course (gray
gossip followed by amber chasers); but had
not passed to the next game level, because he
did not know which button to push.
Last week he tried a red one and dropped too
much money for one night; a green button got
a lot of unanswered calls --
"You look down.
You sound low".

Outside, London was darkly secret, openly cruel;

as two men doss down in a doorway at next
house. One street over dogs cowed in a walled
yard, alone and confused. Further away a fretting
child went to early bed with an unhappy mother.

Inside the tavern it was noisy but not cheerful --
outside, silent but not peaceful (two pigeons lit on
a window sill, blinking at night lights and calling
at traffic). Inside, the bar was warm but not cosy
-- outside, it was cool but not fresh.
Inside their saloon, voices worked well and drinks
sold high, to pairs of men who sit long and hard
in opposing seats trying another round of evening
banter, talk-an-tell…
Outside people go home, children sleep and pets
curl-up to wait.

No. 48

"I take two weeks, maybe three" he said,
"finishing a new poem. So, calculate the
volume will be in the post by mid April" –
I kept sipping medium sherry in his rooms at
Bayswater, because he was an Oxford man,
the man to beat.
He waved off my remarks and reached at
the bottle on the table; an oddment from
his grocer, proven by ordeal.
"What school
you in now" came next? My answer, again,
did not matter. He wanted footnotes, indexed
queries and clever cribs; I was meant to be
artful novice of the parish. Together we sifted
thru a folio of anecdotes/notes/malice and
merit -- like bottom-feeders at a flea market.
By 2pm
it was warm and appealing outside when luck
had it our drinking was over. He had a head like
Homer, greyed and bowed like a museum piece.
I was loathe to consider my own profile by then
as anything than photogenic, not a subject for
molding plaster.
When finally tired of our windy exchanges he
got ahead of me to the door and cast the closing
comments; I never won last words.
Going home was re-joining the wider world
of more people over books, more action than

thought; after three measures of Madeira and two hours of lit-crit versus lit-gossip, enough rations for remaining term time.

No. 49

He spied a new friend this morning --
and came straight over after picking
me out of passers-by and got us into
an awkward handshake.
George, was in the Guards, he said.
"Yuh can't believe it now" he grimaced,
"but I was".
Too pre-occupied to respond in kind,
mailing urgent legal stuff in the post box
before hurrying to my lessons;
he let his chums take him down the street
to find an unused doorway.
They settle to a hard day's drinking at
9-am, as I pass again
and George shouts out, "I really was; the
Royal Life Guards – yeah, see me now",
as he salutes everyone.
"Ask my C.O., Major Ferguson;
he'll tell yuh", with his brave grin again.
I reminded him of better days,
I looked like his officers or something.
He reminded me how life makes no deals
-- good soldiers are forgotten and clever
letters lost in piles of paper.

No. 50

On a bus, top front seat,
I am overviewing the territory.
It is late going home from my job
through crowds and traffic,
desperate and tired.
I am many feet above people
and cars, but I am more
than tired more than desperate
-- angry and violent!
As I descend to the streets
I push and shove with malice and
relish. I tread on toes and
leave old ladies in the dust.
From the bus I saw two men on
the pavement begging.
As I stepped past them I threw
into the hat, not money but bible
tracts and old bus tickets.
I am becoming a tiger and
this is the carcass.

No. 51

I sat on the front step again
with coffee/biscuits,
for access to the street and
wayfarers; access to the news
and talk, sun/air...
It is morning break
from daily chores and such.
Yet this is important drama at
a kerb: connections and snubs,
leers and more props with
children/pets.
No post came (11:00am);
but I had an early start, quiet and
busy – coming to the middle
of day when I am the centre of
attention; as everyone on the street
passes before me, if they want
to or not.

Epilogue

Leaving London
is like leaving your parents -- you must go,
but how and where!?
I keep thinking of early days in the city;
how it was good like childhood and lasted
a long time: the theatre/ old parks/ bursting
crowds.

Now I must go --
but remember the first drunk accosting us
in Leicester Square; a new kind of destitution
for me. He was on the London stage alright,
though not quite on a theatre stage.
He found his audience, myself and two dumb
Yankees; then hit us for change and attention
with his milky vomit, enduring rags and his tag
label (well past sell-by-date).

I must go --
yet will miss even the Liverpool Street station,
a glossy live event any day; real and electric for
thousands traversing the station arena, like players
on a game board.
In August, I miss the throngs of people making
my park over-to a beach front with canvas chairs,
picnics, ball games.
In Winter, I miss staying in for eager callers,
dragging off to church and boarding-up the needs

for another year.

Must go --
after jogging across royal parks on my way home
from Westminster to Bayswater, from first job to first
lodgings.
Those early years when I visited everywhere like
a real tourist.
Swimming the Serpentine Lido in school hols,
performing like an aquarium orca and cricket
among the trees in Kensington evening Gardens.

Go --
after twenty years in school, thousands of teens
'getting my goat', laying in wait to trip and trick;
then rousing staff parties with best trifle and prize
toasting/roasting.
Ten years of home-making at Nottinghill, to host
Friday dinners Sunday teas for the unlikely rag-tags
of my acquaintance. After merriment and tears, love
and loss… work, a child, a book.

Did go --
because I had no Third Act to follow, no final scenes
to take part in. My character was hauled off-stage, off
the pay-roll.
Old friends took new jobs, critics panned my stuff,
family disowned me, the public uninterested -- Finis.

NOTES

"Londinium": is the old Roman name (Latin) for London. It was a fort on the Thames River crossing, far down-stream as possible; subordinate at that time to York and Chester.

No.2   Charles Dickens was the famed Victorian novelist, from 1812-1870; living and working within the city.

No.6   "Acapulco Gold": a registered US trade mark, in 1970's, for a marijuana cigarette product. "Joy of Sex/Cooking" were top-selling book products (also 1970's).

No.9   "Water, water, everywhere, ne any drop to drink" is from 'The Rime of the Ancient Mariner' by S.T.Coleridge; where men thirst but sea-water is slaked.

No.10   Carl Sandburg was an American poet from the Mid-West, 1878-1967. He wrote the famous "Chicago" poem and I chose to follow his form closely, to sketch London. John Betjeman was a popular modern English poet; William Wordsworth a Romantic poet.

No.11   Kensington is a Royal Borough in West London; a large area of residence, parks, stores

(Harrods), hotels(Hilton), colleges, churches and museums… Earls Court is a lively area of South Kensington, popular with young visitors.

A 'Rotten borough' had an unfair representation in Parliament; because of fewer votes, yet many more seats in government; till the 1832 Reform Act.

'Mansion chamber' is a stately room with high ceiling, a feature of Victorian housing; often converted into low-cost studio rentals. Coleridge was a Romantic poet; where in "The Rime of the Ancient Mariner" a troubled seafarer must tell his tale to the wedding guest.

No.13   John Keats, another Romantic poet, from London, 1795-1821; living in many locations, including this splendid house.

No.14   The 'underground tube', or subway, is a transit service for the larger metropolis.

No.15   The 'mad hatter', a renown character from Lewis Carroll in "Alice's Adventures in Wonderland", holds an amazing tea party.

No.16   Portobello is a famous market street, near to Lansdowne Road and Ladbroke Square in Nottinghill; a popular area of North Kensington. Observatory Gdns. is South Ken; Trellick Towers are flats in North Ken; and the Round Pond is in

Ken.Gdns.

No.17   Kensington Gardens is a lovely public park, in West London and was private grounds for the palace. It is a popular place with water, recreation and great 18[th]century tree landscaping.

No.19   Windsor Park is a big recreation area up the Thames in Berkshire, part of which is private to the Queen; traditionally for horse-riding exercises and hunting.

No.21   Green Park and Saint James Park are in central London, near to Buckingham Palace; popular recreation places. An 'orangery' is an 17th/18th century structure, to house citrus fruits; a large one in Ken.Gdns.

No.24   An oxford jacket is a woollen weave with natural colours and county style. Bayswater is a Victorian residence area north of Hyde Park; the fountains draw from an underground stream which flows into the Serpentine Lake.

No.26   W.H.Auden was a modern British poet, 1907-73.

No.28   Fulham is a residence area, with older terraced housing, west of Chelsea and south of Hammersmith.

No.32   Westbourne Grove is a long front of Asian stores/eating places; Queensway, a non-stop shopping street in W2.

No.33   Suicides were a problem for the London Underground; till recent years when trains were not allowed to race into stations, but stopped just before the platform.

No.34   Mayfair is an exclusive section of West London, with clubs and hotels.

No.36   'Barristers chambers' are offices for lawyers serving at Court; prominent are medieval (Tudor) premises at Temple courtyards near to The Strand.

No.38   G.Plimpton was an important New York journalist; editor of 'The Paris Review'.

No.39   Sloane Square is in Chelsea; expensive apartments and stores.

No.42   'Three Men in a Boat' by J.K.Jerome, an amusing tale of three luckless friends on the river at Richmond.
'Mr.Polly' by H.G.Wells, is a dyspeptic character of sad misfortune.
"Water, water…" from 'The Rime of the Ancient Mariner'.

"I could be bound…" from Shakespeare's 'Hamlet', in an early scene.

No.43   Edgware Road Station is on Edgware Rd, up from Marble Arch. Paddington, just off Edgware Rd, centers round the famous railway station.

No.44   There was a solar eclipse over London, summer/99.

No.45   Ontario is a large province in central Canada.

No.46   Trebovir Road leads from Earls Court arena to the station and Nevern Square, behind, overlooks a large garden space.

No.48   Homer was the ancient Greek poet, author of "Ulysses".

EPILOGUE   Leicester Square is 'theatre land' in the West End; Liverpool Street station a major terminus near the financial district; Westminster is the central borough including Parliament and the two cathedrals.
The Lido is a summer swimming area on the Serpentine lake.

AUTHOR

Stuart Newton came over from Canada (Vancouver) after college and up from central California before that, where the poetry interest began. But grew-up in the UK (Northeast) and started with farming work after school in Yorkshire/Northumbria; then onto RAC at Cirencester on the Cotswolds. A school teacher whilst in London, for twenty years, happily residing at Nottinghill -- and had a full life of work, family and friends.

In 1997 became a member of 'Mensa' and wrote lots of short articles on current events and a long article on teaching. This is a fifth book of poems; written very quickly one year, after tripping over new verse material (No.5) on way to a job interview. Now safely occupied with fiction and such-like, thinking the muse has departed away…

Lightning Source UK Ltd.
Milton Keynes UK
05 October 2009

144547UK00001B/12/P